AMAZING MILITARY MACHINES

TANKS AND OTHER MILITARY VEHICLES

by Mari Schuh

PEBBLE
a capstone imprint

Published by Pebble, an imprint of Capstone
1710 Roe Crest Drive, North Mankato, Minnesota 56003
capstonepub.com

Copyright © 2023 by Capstone. All rights reserved. No part of this publication may be reproduced in whole or in part, or stored in a retrieval system, or transmitted in any form or by any means, electronic, mechanical, photocopying, recording, or otherwise, without written permission of the publisher.

Library of Congress Cataloging-in-Publication Data
Names: Schuh, Mari C., 1975- author.
Title: Tanks and other military vehicles / Mari Schuh.
Description: North Mankato, Minnesota : Published by Pebble, an imprint of Capstone, [2023] | Series: Amazing military machines | Includes bibliographical references. | Audience: Ages 5-8 | Audience: Grades K-1 | Summary: "Militaries need tough fighting machines on land. Tanks and other vehicles roll through deserts and speed through rugged mountains to get the job done!"— Provided by publisher.
Identifiers: LCCN 2021059227 (print) | LCCN 2021059228 (ebook) | ISBN 9781666350319 (hardcover) | ISBN 9781666350357 (paperback) | ISBN 9781666350395 (pdf) | ISBN 9781666350470 (kindle edition)
Subjects: LCSH: Tanks (Military science)—Juvenile literature. | Vehicles, Military—Juvenile literature.
Classification: LCC UG446.5 .C58 2013 (print) | LCC UG446.5 (ebook) | DDC 623.74/7—dc23/eng/20211207
LC record available at https://lccn.loc.gov/2021059227
LC ebook record available at https://lccn.loc.gov/2021059228

Image Credits
Shutterstock: Filmbildfabrik, 5, 15, Karasev Viktor, 19, M-SUR, Cover, Mrs_ya, 20, 21 (bottle caps), offstocker, 20-21 (egg carton), paranut, 20 (paper roll), Roman Yanushevsky, 17; U.S. Air Force photo by Staff Sgt. Matthew Smith, 11; U.S. Army photo by Staff Sgt. Jason Hull, 6; U.S. Marine Corps photo by Cpl. Luis A. Vega/ Released, 16; Wikimedia: Public Domain, 9, 13, U.S. Army Europe photo by Visual Information Specialist Markus Rauchenberger/released, 7

Editorial Credits
Editor: Erika L. Shores; Designer: Dina Her; Media Researcher: Jo Miller; Production Specialist: Tori Abraham

All internet sites appearing in back matter were available and accurate when this book was sent to press.

TABLE OF CONTENTS

Tough Tanks 4

Leopard 2 Tank 6

Armored Combat Earthmover 8

Combat Ambulance 10

Superav 12

PUMA 14

Unimog 16

Typhoon 18

   Make Your Own
   Land Vehicle 20

   Glossary 22

   Read More 23

   Internet Sites 23

   Index 24

   About the Author 24

Words in **bold** are in the glossary.

TOUGH TANKS

Tanks and other land vehicles are strong and tough. They drive on rough land. They cross rivers and go up hills. These vehicles carry **cargo**. They also carry troops and help keep them safe.

LEOPARD 2 TANK

This tough tank is covered in thick **armor**. It protects the four crew members inside. Special cameras help the crew see well in the dark.

The crew may need to quickly escape from the tank. It has a hidden door in the floor. The crew can exit the tank there.

ARMORED COMBAT EARTHMOVER

Earthmovers help troops by moving dirt, sand, and rocks. They knock down walls. They clear roads. Earthmovers help dig ditches too.

These vehicles travel on strong tracks. The driver uses a **joystick** to control the vehicle. A camera helps the driver see what is ahead.

COMBAT AMBULANCE

Combat ambulances carry troops who are hurt. These vehicles are built to be tough. They climb steep, hilly areas. They travel across shallow rivers. They travel in all kinds of weather too.

Is help needed far away? A helicopter uses a sling to carry the ambulance there.

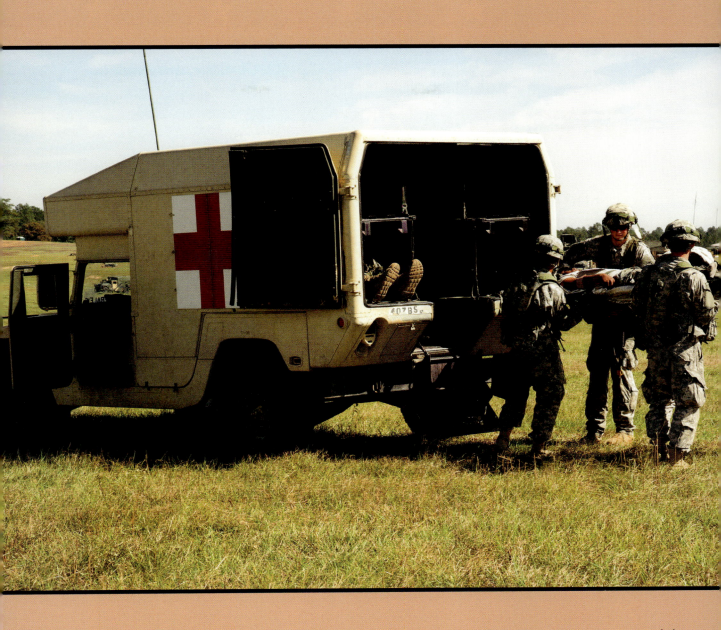

SUPERAV

The Superav is **amphibious**. It travels on land and in water. A **diesel** engine gives it power on land. It is **turbocharged**. The Superav can reach speeds of 65 miles (105 kilometers) per hour.

Two propellers in the back give it power when it's in water. It travels up to 6 miles (10 km) per hour in water.

PUMA

The PUMA works well in all sorts of weather. Very cold or very hot days are no problem for this vehicle.

This strong vehicle keeps troops safe. It protects them from **mines** and other dangers.

UNIMOG

Countries around the world use the Unimog. This military truck carries troops and cargo. It drives on bumpy, uneven ground.

The driver's seat is up high from the ground. This helps keep the driver safe. It also helps the driver see better.

TYPHOON

Typhoon vehicles are covered in strong armor. The seats are made to keep people safe from outside dangers. Five cameras allow drivers to see in all directions.

A Typhoon can go on long trips. It travels 621 miles (1,000 km) without needing more fuel. It is an amazing vehicle!

MAKE YOUR OWN LAND VEHICLE

Make an army tank or other land vehicle with things you find around your home.

What You Need

- egg cartons
- pasta boxes
- bottle tops
- cardboard tubes of all sizes
- tape

What You Do

1. Arrange the items to make your very own toy vehicle. Many short tubes taped together can be the bottom of a tank.

2. Stack boxes to make a place where troops will sit.

3. See if you can make a vehicle you have never seen before!

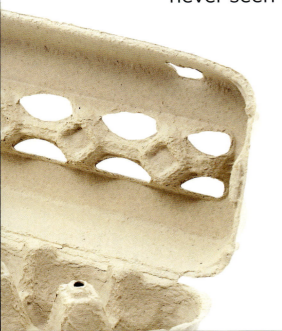

GLOSSARY

amphibious (am-FI-bee-uhs)—able to travel on land and water

armor (AR-muhr)—a heavy metal layer on a military vehicle that protects against bullets or bombs

cargo (KAR-goh)—the goods carried by a tank, ship, aircraft, or other vehicle

diesel (DEE-zuhl)—a heavy fuel that burns to make power

joystick (JOI-stik)—a control stick in a vehicle

mine (MINE)—a type of bomb

turbocharged (TUR-boh-charjd)—having a device that forces air through an engine to make a vehicle go faster

READ MORE

Bassier, Emma. *Military Vehicles*. Minneapolis: DiscoverRoo, an imprint of Pop!, 2020.

Rossiter, Brienna. *Big Machines in the Military*. Lake Elmo, MN: Focus Readers, 2021.

West, David. *Tanks*. New York: Crabtree Publishing Company, 2019.

INTERNET SITES

Kiddle: Tank Facts for Kids
kids.kiddle.co/Tank

Wonderopolis: How Fast Can a Tank Move?
wonderopolis.org/wonder/how-fast-can-a-tank-move

INDEX

armor, 6, 18

armored combat earthmovers, 8

cargo, 4, 16

combat ambulances, 10

Leopard 2 tanks, 6, 7

PUMA, 14

Superav, 12

tanks, 4, 6, 7

Typhoon, 18

Unimog, 16, 17

ABOUT THE AUTHOR

Mari Schuh's love of reading began with cereal boxes at the kitchen table. Today, she is the author of hundreds of nonfiction books for beginning readers. Mari lives in the Midwest with her husband and their sassy house rabbit. Learn more about her at marischuh.com.